July 2024
ISBN-13: 979-8-9855592-7-9

Blind By Dawn

Selected Poems

JEFFREY CHARLES
KINARD

To Anika

Acknowledgements

Originally published in
The FEAST
A Creative Collection, July 2024
Empty Streets
Lunchy Teeth
In The Scrum
Whisper

First published by
In Parentheses, Volume 8, Issue 4
Visiting Is Nice
In America
The Morrow Morn

BLIND BY DAWN

Somewhere the Sun	1
The Crows	2
New Summer Fun	4
Promise You	6
World's an Awful Place	8
Blinking	9
The Parasite	10
Dreamt I Was	12
Gift from the Ghost Girl	13
Known the Nymphs	14
Lady in the Meadow	16
Flowers In Fall	17
Dance The Jig	18
Unique	20
Lazy River	21
Thought You Loved Me	22
Flower Trampled	23
Iron Tear	24
Broken Birds	25
Unseen	26
Empty Streets	27
Alina	28

All My Spirits	30
Lunchy Teeth	31
Walks Like a Crow	32
Ice Cube	34
Ensnared	35
Only My Footsteps	36
Taste My Mistakes	37
In The Scrum	38
Unwilling	40
Visiting is Nice	41
Whisper	42
My Empty Head	43
'til I Disappear	44
See Your Face	45
May Flowers Keep You	46
The Morrow Morn	47
Unnamed	48
The Door to Leave	49
Hinter	50
Immerse	51
In America	52

Blind By Dawn
Selected Poems

Somewhere the Sun

Somewhere the sun is still shining
in a green world after the rain
With snow on the mountains
and love in the fountains
Beyond all the darkness and pain

I'm nestled here with my shadows
We cannot go back where we came
Beneath flowering meadows
I am lying fallow
hoping it won't be my grave

I have a dream of awaking
Of rising again like the dawn
Covered in earth
like a dirty rebirth
Walking into the sun moving on

Somewhere the sun is still shining
in a green world after the rain
With snow on the mountains
and love in the fountains
Beyond all the darkness and pain

The Crows

I dream of all
    the forest green
I cannot find
    the door to leave
I hope the sunshine
    sets me free
The crows
The crows
They're deafening

When dreams go dark
    I fall to sleep
My bed is soft
    the mud is deep
I can't escape
    There's no release
The crows
The crows
They're deafening

The crows
The crows
They know

They know
I am in woe
Buried six feet below

Shadows unfolding
    into wings
They lift off quick
    into the breeze
I twitch and groan
    a damaged thing
The crows
The crows
They rescue me

I dream of all
    the forest leaves
The green below
    rolls like the sea
The sun is all
    we ever need
The crows
The crows
They know

New Summer Fun

It's too much
You make me
holler
Wet and shiver
Hot and bothered

Worship me
You make me
holy
Forget you
Think of me only

>All of this
>new summer fun
>I have just
>begun to come
>Hopefully
>I will last longer
>then this pile of
>silver dollars

I've been down
this road
before
I take it all
and still want more

>All of this
>new summer fun
>I have just
>begun to come
>Hopefully
>I will last longer
>then this pile of
>silver dollars

> I've lost control
> I'm 'round the corner
> Breaking up
> I cannot hold her
> Breaking up...
> Broken

I like the whip
I like the
collar
I like my pile of
silver dollars

Promise You

Eyes aglow
Bodies near skeletal
I promise you
we'll leave this world

Knees and elbows scraped
Every voice enraged
I'm ready for the flood
open the gates

> I promise you
> none of this is true
> We suffer until released

> I promise you
> you'll know what to do
> the moment we slip free

Hair a mess
Barely bother to get dressed
I haven't got
a dollar to my name

The kitchen's full of ants
Searching through the trash
I can't recall
when I last ate

> I promise you
> none of this is true
> We suffer until released

I promise you
you'll know what to do
the moment we slip free

I swear I never loved this place
You and I
our hearts as soft as saints
You and I
we share a simple plan
Live as beasts
and escape the pain of man

Eyes aglow
Bodies near skeletal
I promise you
we'll leave this world

World's an Awful Place

Something caught my eye
Stalking in the dark
I did not but stare
Growling fills the air

> The world's an awful place
> I still like it here
> Darkness may prevail
> But I will walk with fear

Out there in the night
We wander without homes
Our souls are laid so bare
Not but hair and bones

> The world's an awful place
> I still like it here
> Darkness may prevail
> But I will walk with fear

The wolf it shows its face
Shaking now with rage
The world's an awful place
I still like it here

Blinking

Sounds like something's trying
claw up through the floor
I'm in bed not tired
I'm not sleeping anymore

Movement in the shadows
I see nothing more
Think something once hunted here
in what was long before

I sank into my pillow
Dreamt of opening locked doors
What emerged from the darkness
woke me with horror

Blinking
ever closer
in the moment
my eyes close

Blinking
it can see me
in the moment
I'm exposed

Hunting through the darkness
It can see me when I blink
and I see it getting closer
I cannot move I cannot think

Something's looking for me
I opened the door
I'm in bed not tired
I'm not sleeping anymore

The Parasite

The parasite
is sympathetic
Gives me what I need

Something stranger
rare and different
A thriving malady

   Such a joy
   a pleasure synapse
   rings with clarity

   Try to kick
   give in and relapse
   The parasite digs deep

Take from me
my day's desires
Take my will to be

Anything
all rapt with pleasure
Please don't ever leave

   Chemicals
   I want them all
   coursing through my veins

   Seep into
   the hidden places
   lost inside my brain

I dream the things
I will never do
Dreams do not come true

The parasite
forgets about me
Hope that you do too

Dreamt I Was

Darkness closing in
on another day
The sun is going down
I have lost my way

> Dreamt I had
> a place to go
> Dreamt my life away
>
> Spent my days
> waiting for
> the right spell to say

We end in the night
We die beneath the stars
Nothing that we know
tells us who we are

> Dreamt I was
> someone to know
> Dreamt my life away
>
> Spent my days
> waiting for
> the right spell to say

Dreamt I was
Dreamt I was

GIFT FROM THE GHOST GIRL

Gift from the ghost girl
A lush wisp of dew kiss
All your bright dreams
dissolve in the moon mist

Do you remember?
We had such a good time
rolling in flowers
that bloom in the night

Gift from the ghost girl
Eyes sparkle like champagne
All your troubles
rinse away in the soft rain

Do you remember?
We had such a good time
laughing like lovers
drunk in the vines

Gift from the ghost girl
Her tears pearly opals
All your memories
fade like leaves in the fall

Known the Nymphs

I've known the nymphs
and they still dance
in meadows near
the river path

In mossy glens
they roll and laugh
with growing boys
and men of glass

Got blind drunk
on bending wine
and stumbled
into darker climes

I wandered lost
towards icy stars
To rocky peaks
high, dry, and far

> I know a woman
> who knows well her womb
> Whose senses swell
> with the glowing moon
>
> Child of the Sun
> how dark your love
> Bless the bliss
> that makes us one

I am bearded
I am scarred
My wild heart wrapped
in something hard

Each breath I take
is like a spell
Each moment ringing
like a bell

> I know a woman
> who knows well her womb
> Whose senses swell
> with the glowing moon
>
> Child of the Sun
> how dark your love
> Bless the bliss
> that makes us one

Lady in the Meadow

Tell me something better
then warm weather in the spring
Flowers all around her
Mushrooms growing in a ring

All the trees are talking
to the birds and to the breeze
I'm waiting for a woman
A good omen from the east

> Lady in the meadow
> Sunshine shattered by the leaves
> If you catch me watching
> then I know you're not a dream

I dare you to kiss me
in the shadows of the vines
Twisting round my shoulders
and clutching to my thighs

I have been here watching
in my long eternal night
Never thought I'd see a sunrise
Never thought I'd see the light

> Lady in the meadow
> Sunshine shattered by the leaves
> If you catch me watching
> then I know you're not a dream

Flowers In Fall

Grass grown so tall
Flowers in fall
Warm still the orange
    setting sun

I am in love
The idea of love
I hope I have met
    the right one

All the butterflies
All the million insect eyes
watching my time
    slip by

A dancing gold halo
lights up the humming meadow
Oh love it's been
    so long

So long since
    I've dared to love

Dance The Jig

Never known where I am going
I've been to interesting places
Far off from the well-trod path
I've known so many faces

I claim the starlight as my own
No one else seems to be looking
I'm staring out into the night
with perpetual poor footing

> I dance the hustle
> I dance the jig
> I'm falling through
> tight openings

> Still here today
> Here today

Never known what could've helped me
I was thrown and always falling
There were times I thought I found a home
but I was only stalling

Perhaps I could have been like you
Pretending I am flying
to some place extraordinary
I'm just no good at lying

I dance the hustle
I dance the jig
I'm falling through
tight openings

Still here today
Here today

If we ever meet again
I'll consider myself lucky
to recognize a long lost friend
along this empty highway

Unique

Upstate
where the flowers grow
In the calm of the sun
all your damage shows

No one needs to be
more unique

Fill my wounds
with liquid gold
My wrinkles smiling
Stars are old

To be finished is to be
complete

>   And the present rings like a bell
>   resonating across the hills
>   We have all the time we have
>   to be alive
>
>   The past is not with us still
>   unless you bring your buckets filled
>   Then how do you expect to drink now
>   from this well?

Upstate
where the flowers grow
In the calm of the sun
all your damage glows

No one needs to be
more unique

Lazy River

On the lazy river
time unwinds in the sunshine
The birds are keeping busy
Not a dark cloud in the sky

I'm caught in the eddy
turning circles for a time
Some might resort to paddles
but I promised not to try

> You can see the laughing me
> on my way downstream
> I see no need to row my boat
> if life is but a dream

On the lazy river
the nights are never quiet
The insects and the frogs rehearse
parts for the midnight choir

> You can see the laughing me
> on my way downstream
> I see no need to row my boat
> if life is but a dream

Thought You Loved Me

I thought you loved me
I thought you knew all my scars
I thought my darkness
for you was full of stars

I thought my pain and grief
had found release, relief
I thought you loved me

I thought you loved me
Thought I could be myself
I thought my honesty and depth
would lead to greater health

I thought my flaws and kinks
had found release, relief
I thought you loved me

I thought I'd found
the one that I would marry
I thought my heart
had found sanctuary

Although you filled my eyes
you were not ride or die
You didn't love me

Flower Trampled

A flower trampled
in the mud
An open heart
destroyed by love

And here among
the waste I bleed
to barely bloom
and never seed

    I don't know a way
    to avoid any pain
    I step into the fray
    deranged

    I've come all this way
    to lay here in the rain
    All that I have learned
    not to complain

So now upon
deep roots depend
To wait 'til spring
and try again

And here among
my failed attempt
Another chance
to convalesce

Iron Tear

I shed an iron tear
when I remember love
It was another life
It was somewhere up above

And now I sit down here
Alone for half the year
I know the loss of love
I shed an iron tear

I'm known for being fair
but inaccessible
I may remain unseen
Still unforgettable

Look out upon my world
All the lost are here
I give eternal peace
I shed an iron tear

Broken Birds

I lost my way
and my unsure steps
took me back
to my fallen ex

I felt so bad
to feel so sad
But that's just how she left me
She left me

    I fall in love
    with broken birds
    I think I'll help them

    I like that they
    don't fly away
    They are so broken

And when I mend
their broken wings
I am fool enough to think
they love me

They do not love me

I lost my way
and my unsure steps
took me back
to my fallen ex

I felt so bad
to feel so sad
We are still broken

Unseen

When you go
looking for
what goes unseen

You must go
veiled as though
one of those things

Unseen like
shadows like
small living things

Unseen like
a dream life
remembering

Move among
people like
the softest breeze

Hum your song
softly as
all the world sleeps

Today is
the day you
finally see

All that is
hidden here
including me

Empty Streets

I look for you on empty streets
crowded with pale ghosts
I long for feelings long since past
I felt with you the most

I don't believe you'd see me
if by chance we meet again
But I like the dream and cannot leave
the idea we are friends

I wander all these empty streets
crossroads at every block
Where mercuries still wait for me
to reset all the clocks

There was a time there was still time
before all time had stopped
I cannot leave these empty streets
until you're truly lost

Alina

Tonight I dreamt
of bright Alina
tracking starlight
through the snow

Dark woods scratch
the aching gray sky
Will they ever
let her go?

Catch a teardrop
as she passes
Can I touch her?
Reach her ghost?

Would she wake up
from her trance state?
Would she burst
like a cloud of smoke?

I think of all
I'd like to give her
Call to her
She does not hear

Her hands reach out
for what I don't know
Watch her slowly
disappear

Today I'm eating
all the clouds
The sun streams in
to melt the ground

The dark woods swell
Explode with green
Alina gone
Fond memory

All My Spirits

I've been calling
all my spirits in
My spirits in
to me

Sometimes wonder
what they think of me
I've never been
so clean

> I have urges
> I've depravity
> I have dreams
> no one should see
>
> I'm not being
> what I think would please
> all the spirits
> around me

I've been calling
all my spirits in
If they don't like me
guess they'll leave

I think they know
I am just human
and they were once
like me

Lunchy Teeth

Lunchy teeth
mash a pasty meal
Licking tongues
leave the lips to feel

the crumbs of corners
Saliva drips
trickle down
on fingertips

Filthy nails
crawl from plate to face
Sopping wet
with fat and grease

Satisfied
the lunchy teeth
swallow gobs
of steaming feast

Walks Like a Crow

Walks like a crow
foot shoulders back
Sliding along
a meandering path

Where he has been
most don't come back
Down where the source
flows raw and black

> Takes one to know one
> don't it, Jack?
> Who's he think he is
> to walk like that?

After the fire
he returned intact
Nub like wings
sprouting from his back

Where will he fly
when free at last?
All his desires
melted back to black

> Takes one to know one
> don't it, Jack?
> Who's he think he is
> to walk like that?

Walks like a crow
foot eyes of glass
Searching the sky
for a spell to cast

> Takes one to know one
> don't it, Jack?
> Who's he think he is
> to walk like that?

Ice Cube

The cool of the ice cube
glass full of liquor
Amber gold honey
straight without mixer

I take a deep sip
wipe off my whiskers
I have such a weakness
for such strong elixirs

The life in the bar mirror
so far behind me
People are passing
their smiles to the barmaid

Everyone's talking
over the music
Sounds so emphatic
but it's nothing amusing

The cool of the ice cube
swirling translucent
Taking slow drinks
of this life while I'm lucid

Ensnared

I am ensnared
in my own hunger lair
My passions
I let them take me

Too much letting go
is lazy and I know
I need control

I spring a leak
and I'm sitting in my own juices
The damp debauch
of my basest urges

Hungrier
than ever before

I am ensnared
A master of traps
and the catch
I'm getting bored

ONLY MY FOOTSTEPS

Wasted tonight
on the empty bricks
Broken lamp lights
leave the shadows thick
And echoing wet
through the twisted streets
only my footsteps

Turn of the key
in my building home
Yellow lobby
radiator groan
Climbing the stairway
to a room alone
only my footsteps

Chair and a table
fill an old glass
Fresh sips of whiskey
think of the past
None know my stories
No one on my path
Only my footsteps
and my lonely laugh

Taste My Mistakes

Sip your drink and think
does she still love you?
She doesn't seem to
Doesn't need you

When you're young you need
someone to hang on to
The world was so big
      It's smaller now

    I feel it so loud
    Taste my mistakes
    like blood in my mouth

Growing up is just
learning a routine
Keeping yourself clean
Having no time

I distrust the clock
A face I cannot see through
I used to watch the light
      but I got lost

    I feel it so loud
    Taste my mistakes
    like blood in my mouth

In The Scrum

In the scrum
of hollow places
where I lick my lips await

> the sting of
> sudden endings
> the warm blood
> of lust filled hate

In the din
of luckless donkeys
grinning toothless without wit

> nights grind on
> til wet with yawns
> churning life
> to formless shit

>> Once I knew love
>>> long ago
>> and not my heart
>>> so bright outspoken

>> With love lost
>>> I found my heart
>> as it is now
>>> forever broken

In the scrum
of distant faces
I do not feel out of place

    where the water
    is all whisky
    and our lives
    are our disgrace

Unwilling

Unwilling
to be severe
and growing softer

Comfortable
You forget
our hardships hone us

Where are your trials, your tribulations?
Your sacrificed gains upon the altar?

Stuck in the mood of accumulating
Are you sluggish and squishy, ripe for rot?

Unwilling
to risk it all
here comes the cancer

Spreading through
your spiritual
disaster

Visiting is Nice

I miss being foreigner
in an exotic land
I long to learn new customs
and touch a stranger's hand

I'm tired of the mirror
I'd like another's eyes
reflecting back to me
things I barely recognize

I miss being welcomed in
I long to be a guest
Conscious of my every move
my manner might suggest

I'd like to listen to new sounds
and struggle to make sense
of everything that's said to me
while I fumble to express

I miss letting someone in
my complicated life
who looks around, smiles and says
Visiting is nice

Whisper

I came to whisper
sweet nothings to whiskey
Nibble on mushrooms
Stumble on home

I've been seen weaving
between the tall buildings
Followed by rainstorms
Dry as old bones

I have imagined
that I'm on a pathway
Guided by chances
Beguiled by songs

All paths lead back
to candles and bar stools
Glasses of whiskey
I whisper away

My Empty Head

Times I need a prison
when my monsters
lose control

Times I need a mountain
and a night out
in the cold

Times I need a highway
long horizons
full of sun

Times I need an ocean
when there's nowhere
left to run

Times I need a lover
one to talk me
into bed

Times I need a desert
where I can clear
my empty head

My empty head

'til I Disappear

Someone is crying
I feel their tears
Someone is dying
I face their fears

I am wide open
all of these years
Love after heartache
'til I disappear

Morning comes slowly
nights are so long
Quiet the darkness
heart full of songs

Time is not broken
pulls us along
I try to fight it
but I'm not that strong

Someone is laughing
I float through the air
Someone is napping
dreams without care

All the world glowing
with life while we're here
Love after heartache
'til I disappear

See Your Face

I see your face
You are revealed
I see the moving flesh
express the way you feel

I feel your breath
I feel you breathe
I feel you throb beneath
my fingers feel your heat

And for a while
I don't want you to leave
I want to know you more
than you might believe

Offer my lips
You give your tongue
My hand runs down your neck
to your breasts as you cum

I read your cards
It makes you cry
We eagerly share truths
with seduction in our eyes

And for a while
I don't want you to leave
I want to know you more
than you might believe

May Flowers Keep You

May flowers keep you
tucked away and
sealed with dew

Deep in the embrace
of petals fresh
and new

May breezes sway you
gentle wind chime
lullabies

Soft the touch of
moonlight on your
sleeping eyes

May morning wake you
warm your bones
and bid you rise

Greet the sun
inside my garden
where yesterday you died

The Morrow Morn

The morrow morn
will meet you wiser
so much sadder
than before

When you question
all the answers
that once fortified
your core

When you look
upon existence
fleeting senseless
endless gore

Without the lies
of stories molding
chaos into
something more

The morrow morn
will meet you wiser
so much sadder
and forlorn

But the courage
to face horror
the universe
richly rewards

Unnamed

Shadows in the darkness
gazing back

The whisper in the wind
writes all my songs

Chaos in the branches
says goodbye

The tangle in the vines
by wild design

Every crosstown light
I hit is green

The way before me
opens like a sea

I'm drawn into the current
willfully

Fighting things would only mean
I lose

The Door to Leave

Tangled up
at the end of life
Tired of it all

No longer get
anything I like
The world is much too small

Looking for
the door to leave
Ready to let go

Following
everyone I've loved
Everyone I'll ever know

My whole life
is a cataract
A free fall without end

Once you fall
There's no coming back
Just how long you will pretend

Looking for
the door to leave
Ready to let go

Following
everyone I've loved
Everyone I'll ever know

Hinter

An odd vacancy
eventually filled
with memories and spirits

A place in a dream
where your loved ones
wait on the stairs

Somewhere nearby
shadows converse
like old friends

With each passing
the door creaks
further open

One day
we all return
to the hinter

To compare notes
on the glimmering moment
we remember

Immerse

I don't feel
the flint in words
filling the books
with verse

I may respect
a turn of phrase
An antique doorknob
works

I cannot hear
verse read aloud
without feeling
somehow worse

The draughty place
these words reside
An abandoned house
accursed

Woe the poet
lost in time
reliving all
this murk

An antenna
of our times
must in our times
immerse

In America

In America
the flags are frayed
and there's gum under the tables

In America
the gutters are lined with trash
and the cars are abandoned

The cats and bullets are strays
The railings are greasy
The sidewalks cracked from the roots
of trees now stumps

There's graffiti of hope in the subways
and a mother crying
The sirens never stop
drawing us into cul-de-sacs of depression

In America
the streets are full of bodies
The sky gray with indifference

In America
our shadows are on television
Time is up
and we're sleeping through the alarm